I0827130

ROHHEIT

Poetry

Kitty Barks

Published by Kitty Barks, Anaconda, Montana.

Cover design and interior illustrations by Kitty Barks
Forward by Sarah Samms

Printed in the United States of America

ISBN 978-0-578-60912-6

Library of Congress Control Number: 2019918476

First Edition January 2020

kittybarksart.com

Forward

When Kitty Barks approached me with her debut poetry book, Rohheit, I was honored to have the opportunity to be given a platform to praise this artist of the night. She and I met under the utmost of strange circumstances in a tiny little town in western Montana named Anaconda- where we both lived in a half-abandoned commercial building amongst other artists who didn't have anywhere to go but the collective compound we had created.

Kitty would spend days painting her nightmares onto canvas, depicting raw beauty through cynical light. Her lens to the world in her paintings resonates with many that live life on the other side of the norm. Rohheit is a bellowing echo of her paintings in many ways.

Her raw and real nature comes to light in her poetry with a punch to the gut. Bringing the reader to dark corners of their minds where many don't like to visit. Yet Kitty goes into those dark corners and plays around in the cobwebs, bringing you right along with her. And in those cobwebs lies her dark sense of humor threaded along with her story- shedding light on the shadows of her mind.

The drawings in Rohheit perfectly resonate with the words she carefully smithed onto paper. Aesthetically they are raw, still, and quiet but emotionally they are loud, powerful and bring the reader's heart right where she wants you.

It's been an incredible journey to watch this artist grow in her creative stature over the years but it's been even more incredible watching her grow spiritually. Rohheit is a perfect depiction of her spiritual growth. The ability to humiliate the ego and paint your soul with ink on paper is an incredible feat. Kitty Barks did just that in her debut book, Rohheit. I look forward to reading along as she continues her journey with wordsmithing the nightmares of man and the heart desires of the creatures of the night.

Sarah Samms
Author, Musician, Herbalist

www.SammBones.com

Sarah D. Samms

ROHHEIT

Summary

We never made it
Though how we tried

We thought we would
And then we died

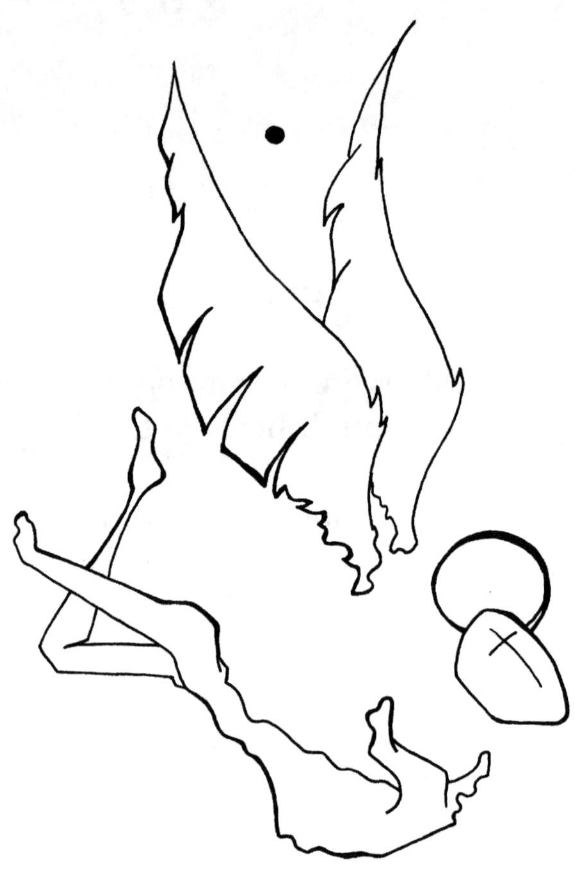

Ideas

Something's waiting in the wings
In quiet nights and shapeless things
Try to lure it close with song
Impatient minds can't wait so long

It paces silent beyond the light
Teasing cruelly just out of sight
Such size is felt in rumbling ground
Though searching ears can find no sound

Forever near but out of grasp
Call for it in dying rasp
As the fire fades we mourn
Weep for creatures never born

Lessons

Ich habe gelernt
Dass die Welt
Sieht mich nicht

Free

The disaffected freedom
Having nowhere to be
Ever somebody's burden
They prefer not to see

The right kind of lonely
For the wrong bet to take
Sleep tight in the alley
Sad sounds shadows make

Time drowns out your heart
When nothing takes it away
It gets in your mouth
And begs you to stay

Deal

You love me
I know it's right
You wouldn't lie
We never fight

You even say it
I've heard it said
You only say it
When I give you head

You love me
It must be true
You repeat it always
When I fuck you

You love me
I make it real
You play your part
Our fucking deal

You wander off
I wonder why
You just need time
I sucked you dry

You do love me
I know it still
You don't come back
I know you will

We had a deal

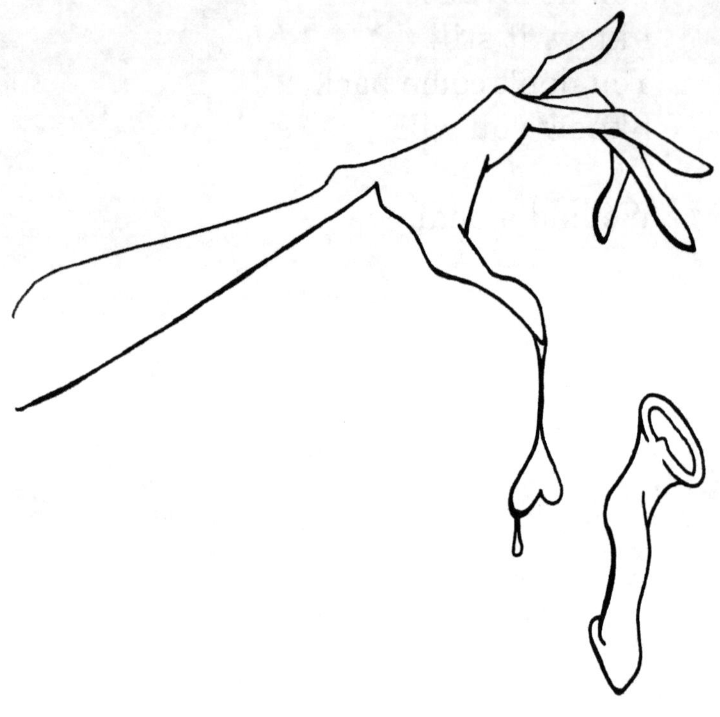

Accountable

There's no justice in forgiving
No redeeming me at all
I alone the only witness
Silent owner of your sickness

I will not let you go
Though it damages me still
If I do it disappears
Even screaming, no one hears

Poetry

I think poetry is stupid
Pretentious
Masturbation

All the shit I write
Terrible
Elementary

If you're reading this
Don't
Please

On knowing

What beauty lies
In word and song
Can poke at meaning
For lifetimes long

But nothing holds
Such weight and scope
As silent knowing
Needless of hope

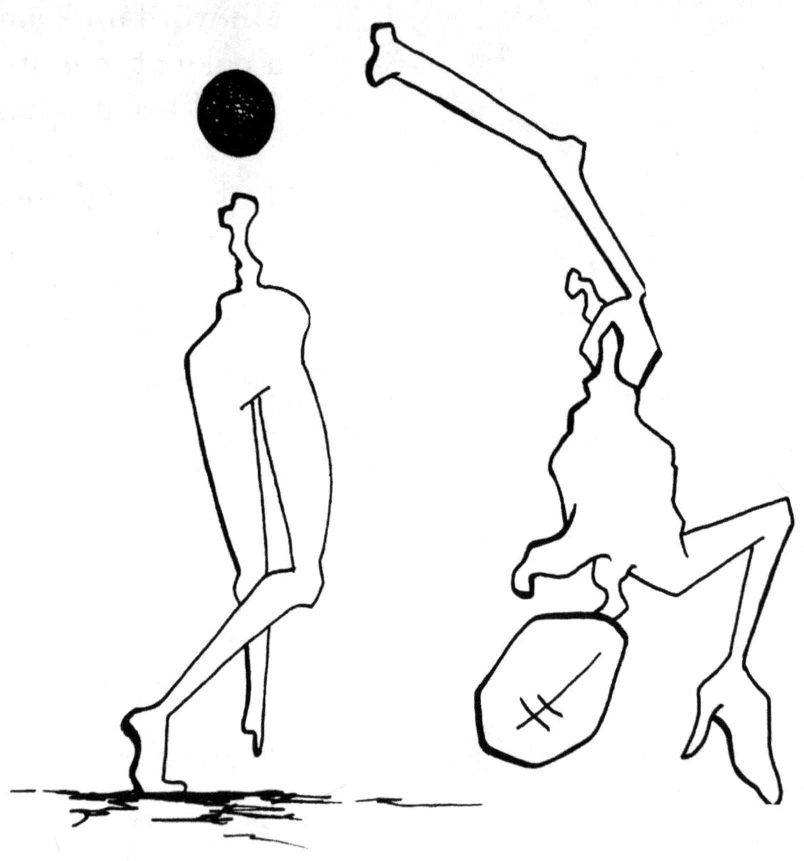

BHS

Body
Getting soft
Make it bleed
Punch a hole
Leave a pool

Heart
Getting cold
Make it hurt
Pry it open
Let it burn

Soul
Getting lost
Make it scream
Salt your wounds
Watch them leak

Audience

No one will see
What falls out of my head
But I did this thing
And now I'm dead

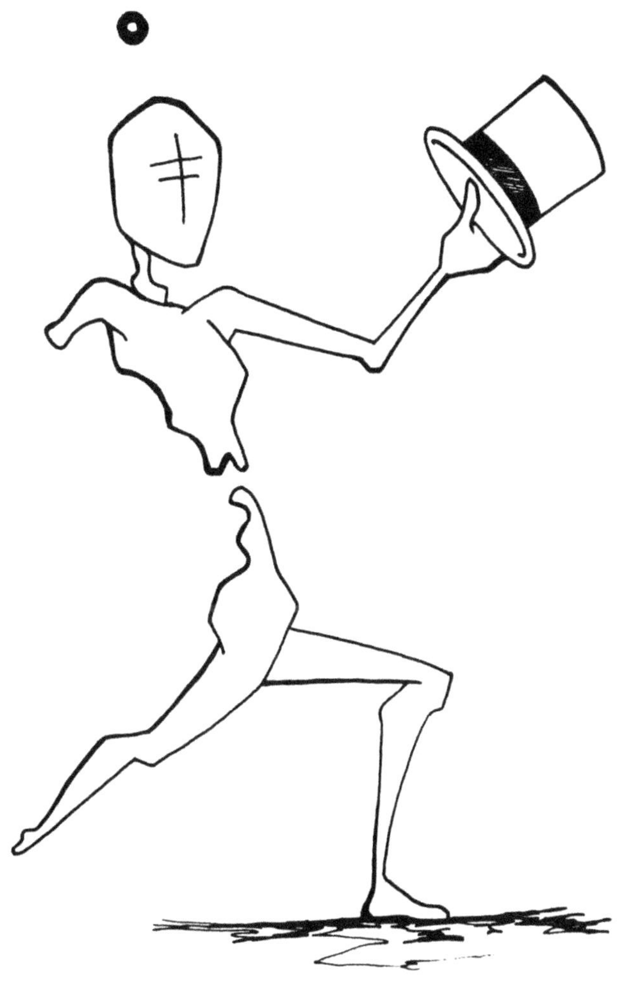

L* / *ATE**

I once knew a love
That's worth killing for
Barely got out
With red on the floor

Don't use such a word
To name your disease
Your hate smiles brightly
When I'm down on my knees

Nine

One digit down
And a thousand miles gone
Take a breath now
Step off the edge

Coagulating gasoline
Slow burn flight
Ever rolling wreck
Let it strike

Beautiful things
Can only make lesser
Shit in the street
Will make something better

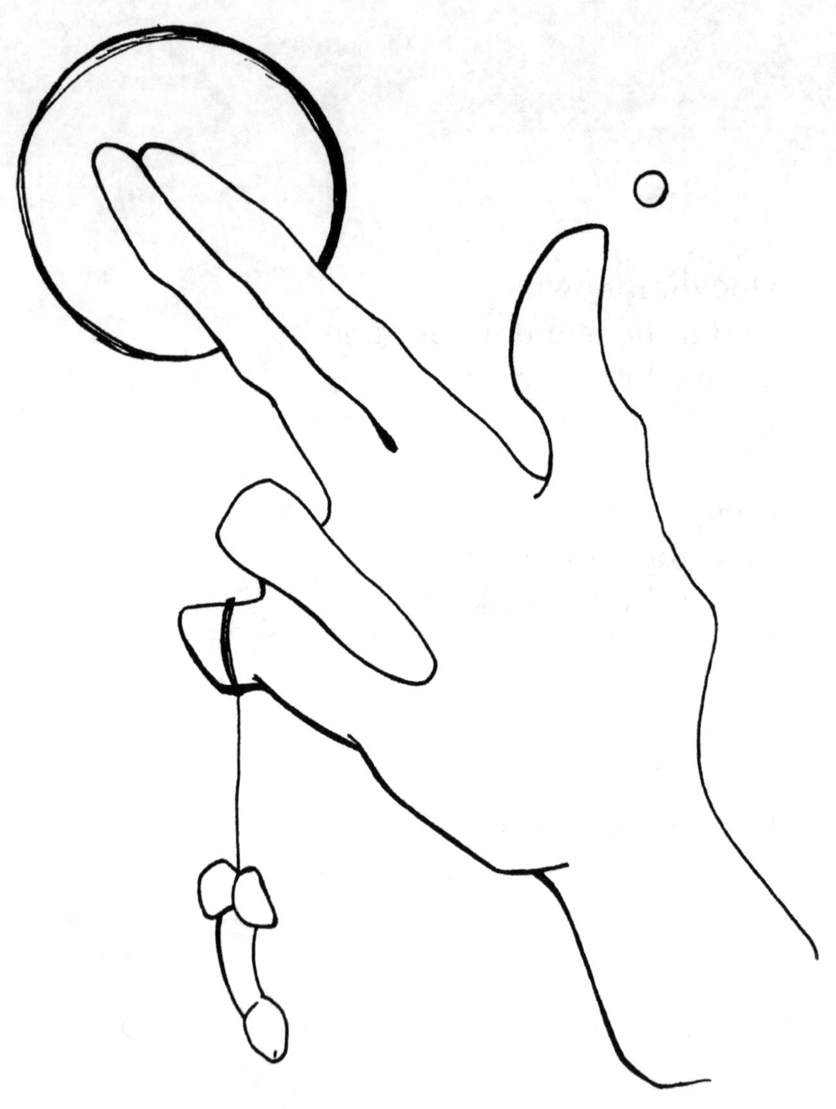

Love letter to Myself

Dumpster fire
You're very pretty
From far away

Trash fire
No one wants you
In their yard

Dumpster fire
Stay over there
We smell you from here

Trash fire
You have your uses
But not any virtues

Dumpster fire
Tell yourself something nice
To get through

Trash fire
You're very pretty
Why thank you

The Cost of Sleeping

Dreams are just
Things you'll never be
All those joys
Are never really free

30

Thirty years a lie
Made me thirty years a liar
Truth blinked its eye
Passed my life entire

Look back on your way
See you know your story
Hope you never see a day
Betrayed by allegory

In a moment life is fiction
Myself a character flat
Though played with much conviction
Not any more than that

What history has hidden
I've seen it now at last
My mind goes unforgiven
For lying to the past

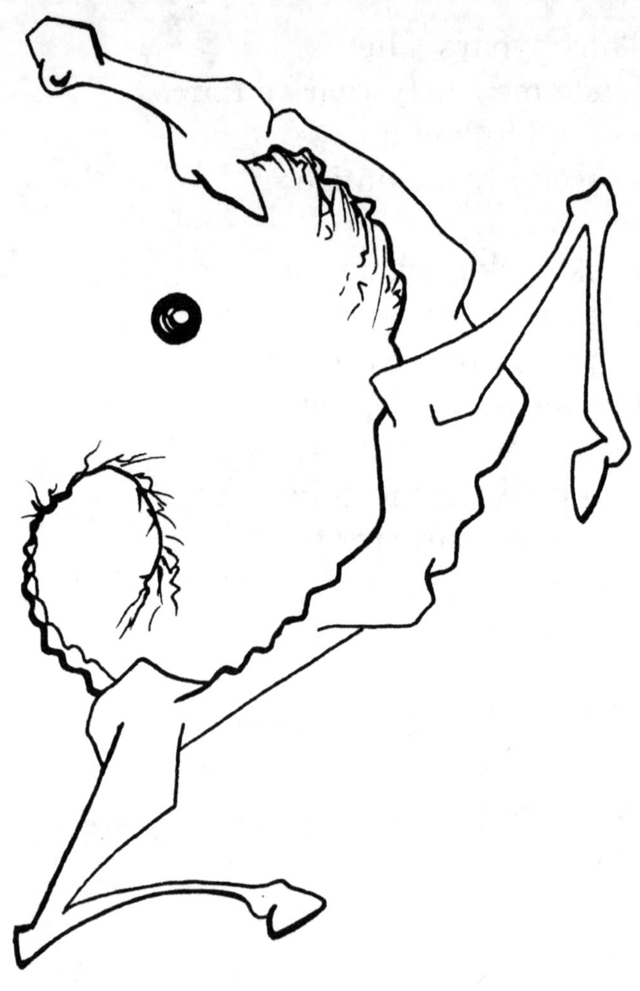

It Begins

Damnation installation
Before the story's dawn
What was meant to be fresh space
Already just too smeared
Finished future from endless chances
Beholden to another's debt
Genetic self-aggression

Happy Accident

No one asked to be here
Wandering in the dark
Purpose driven arbitrary
Searching for the spark

We find ourselves yet living
Though none know really why
Inventing reasons to continue
Knowing it's a lie

Roll along now anyway
Find a happy thing
The truth of it is unimportant
No reason not to sing

Question

Der Hai hat noch die Katze gefragt
Warum magst du das Wasser nicht?
Und die Katze hat es ihm gesagt
Weil Wasser hasst das Licht

Old

Nearly forty years it's been
    Still digging shards out of my skin

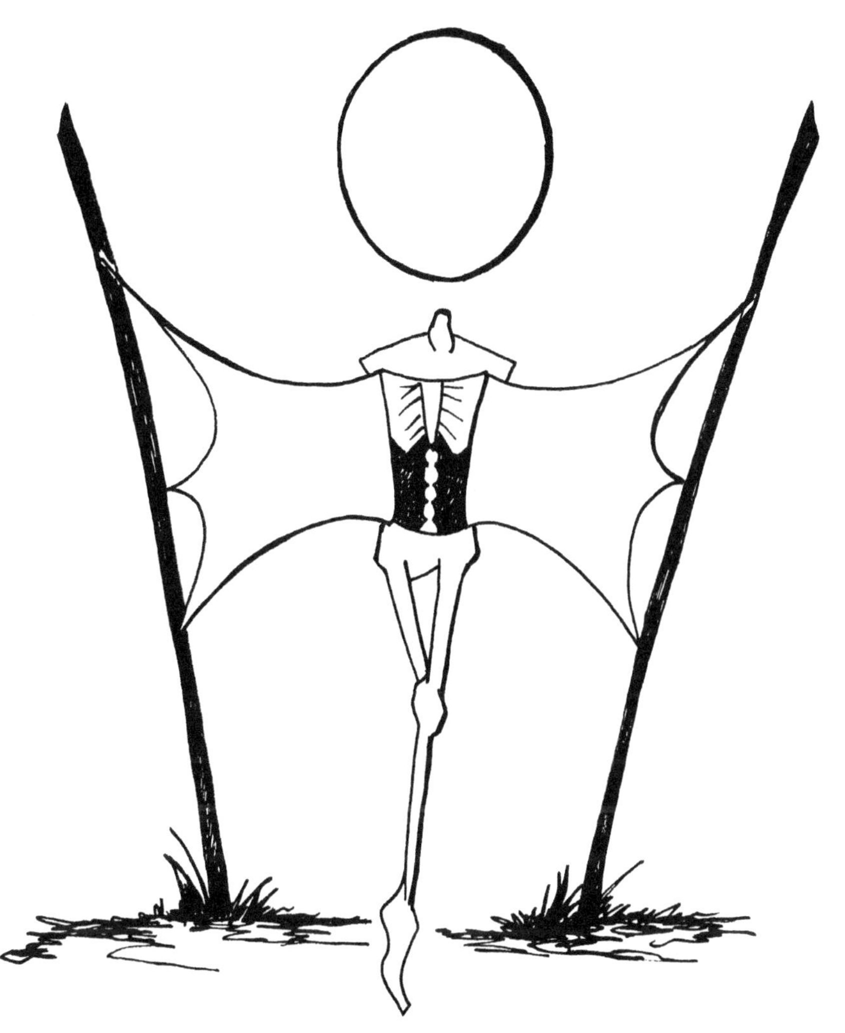

Solitary

Sexually transmitted masochism
Passed down through day and age
Inward rage, outward fear
Baring teeth to bring them near

Smiling, snarling, friend or foe
Tender touch still leaves a bruise
Tangled roots and wilted blooms
Pain sits quiet in darkened rooms

Far away, death or distance
Sticking strings connect you still
We never came, you never left
Half a crime gone unconfessed

Einweg

I swallowed your affection
And wondered where it went
Why the love in your eye had gone
I don't exist when you're content

Your head finds me fascinating
While mind thinks I'm mundane
So I give it about ten minutes
I'm just waiting for the train

Then I'm the one of ones again
For three right minutes I believe
Than I'm something you might want
Or at least be sad to leave

Today I'll take what I can scavenge
Resigning soul to fate
Settle for the crumbs of caring
Single serving mate

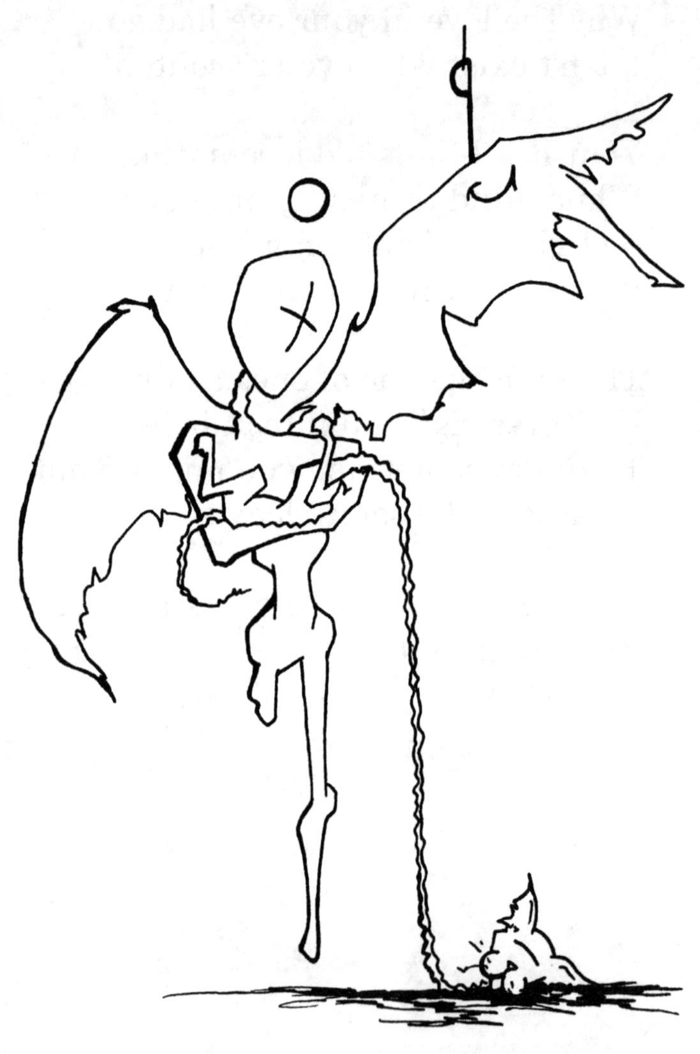

AA

Aimless angels
Wandering in the wind
Faceless fallen
Legends for the sin

Whispers winding
Down roadway and rail
Truth is trying
But stories never fail

Sun and Saturn
Brightness and the dark
Beauty bonded
On trailway to embark

Hellfire and hail
Seven devils in the mind
Running rampant
Another one of kind

Distant directions
No mind to stormy weather
These are colors that can't
Help but run together

Solve

Burn it down
Leave your crown
Laying in the street
Nothing's real
All your zeal
Spent fleeing from defeat
Freedom's found
On the ground
With nothing left but meat
Reaching up
Uncorrupt
Red bleeding sun to greet
Win it back
Heart goes black
Pain driving to compete
Sit content
Recall, lament
When you were sharper and elite
Time for flame
Fuck your name
Now hunger you must beat
Round it turns
For a soul that burns
Living on your feet

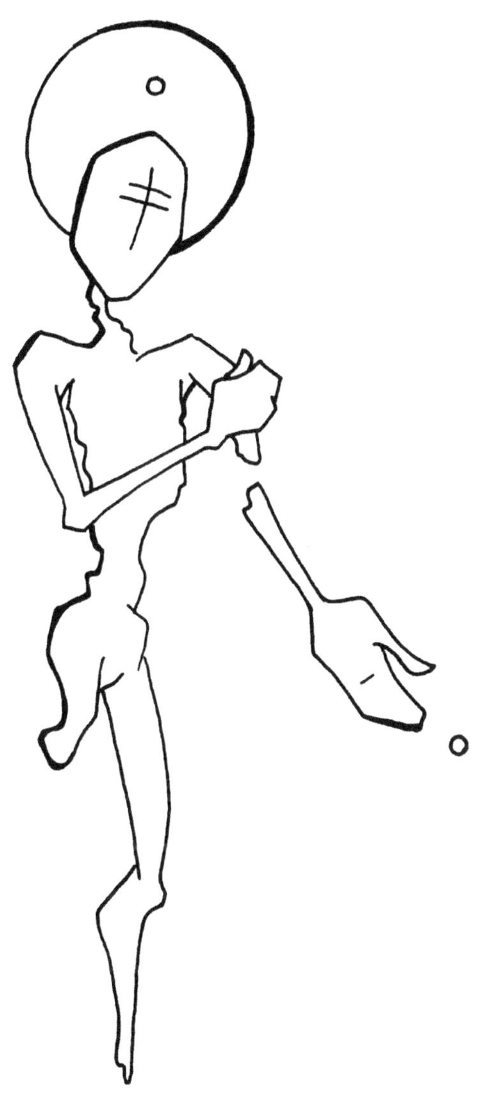

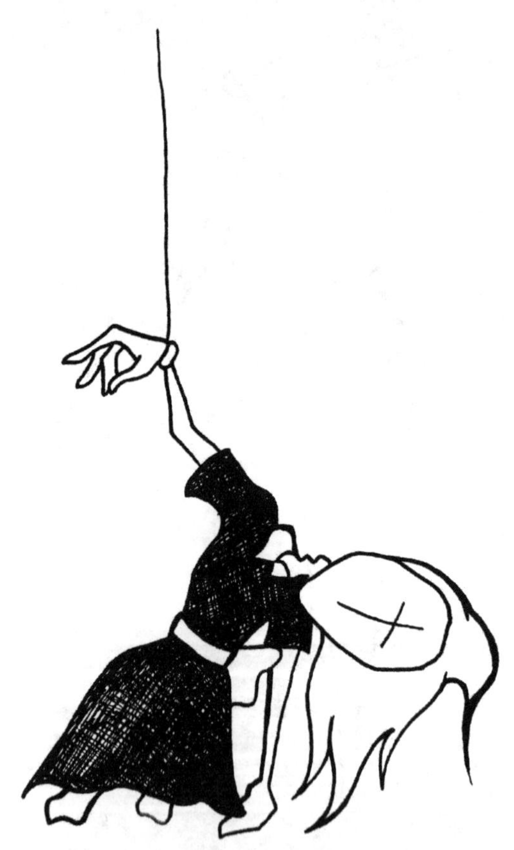

Girl

The most horrific sound
Pray you never hear
A child's cry turning ‘round
From imagination's fear
Toward desperate mourning
For future has already lost
Stolen with a simple warning
Say a word and it will cost

Bore

Diagnosably deficient
Panic without pain
Compulsion for to suffer
Terror tempts what I inflict
Big bore needles
Raw red holes
Considerably masochistic
Played with fine finesse
Distraction from detraction
You could never touch me
The way I touch myself

Emerald

Sixty thousand in a shoebox
Pay farmer Green sly as a fox
Count it quick and cut me in
Time for trimmigration once again
Up the hill where no one looks
Swimmin' in trim, bushes on hooks
Double cross will be your loss
Cliff car graveyard has a spot
A hundred gone without a thought
Get your bank and your bail
Make a break for Reno mail

Gaslamp

With a word you make me
Disbelieve
You must be right because
I'm made wrong
You've stolen all the pieces
The game cannot be played
What's left now
Never was right before
You said I was trying
To be a disaster
Overplaying the past
Meaningless martyrdom
How many stitches
Will suffice
To convince you that
I was never at play
You didn't believe
The blood on the floor
Now you wonder why
I don't answer anymore
Go ahead and tell yourself
That you know me well

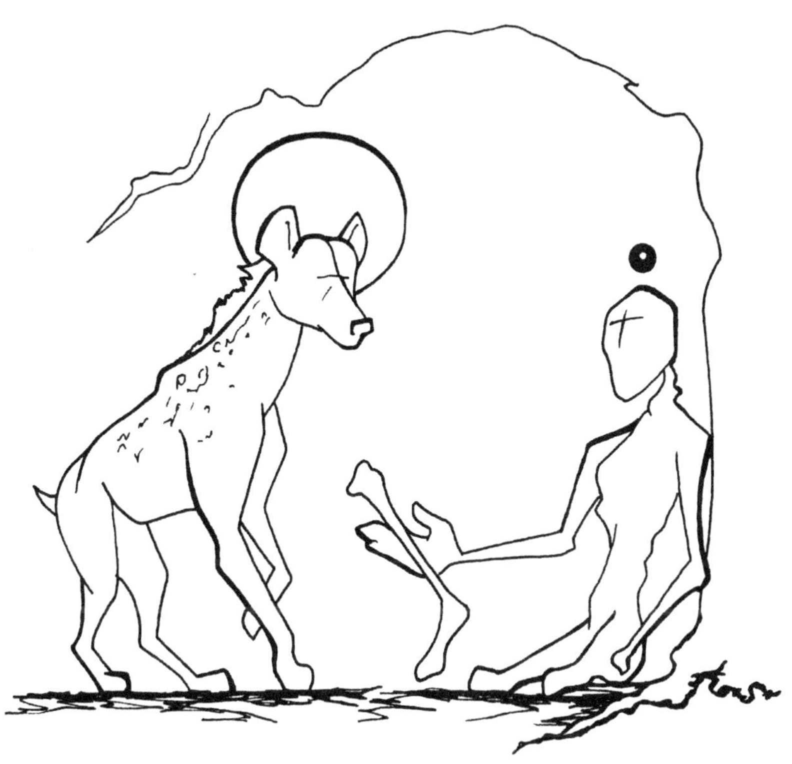

Naught

Howling at the past
It doesn't say a thing
The void
Inseparably internal
Swallowed before the daybreak
Hollow stone at the core
Inhale the deep but cannot drown
Crushing nothing
Inward out
He says silent
Vox will not

Self-Deception

We're all just trying
To manufacture something lasting
Poking sticks at permanence
Tell yourself it will make the mark
Engrave the legend
Echo the story
Stop time marching on
Freeze you there
At the time you touched forever
Pretend you can live right there
Where endings were too far to hear
It's the only way
To keep from screaming

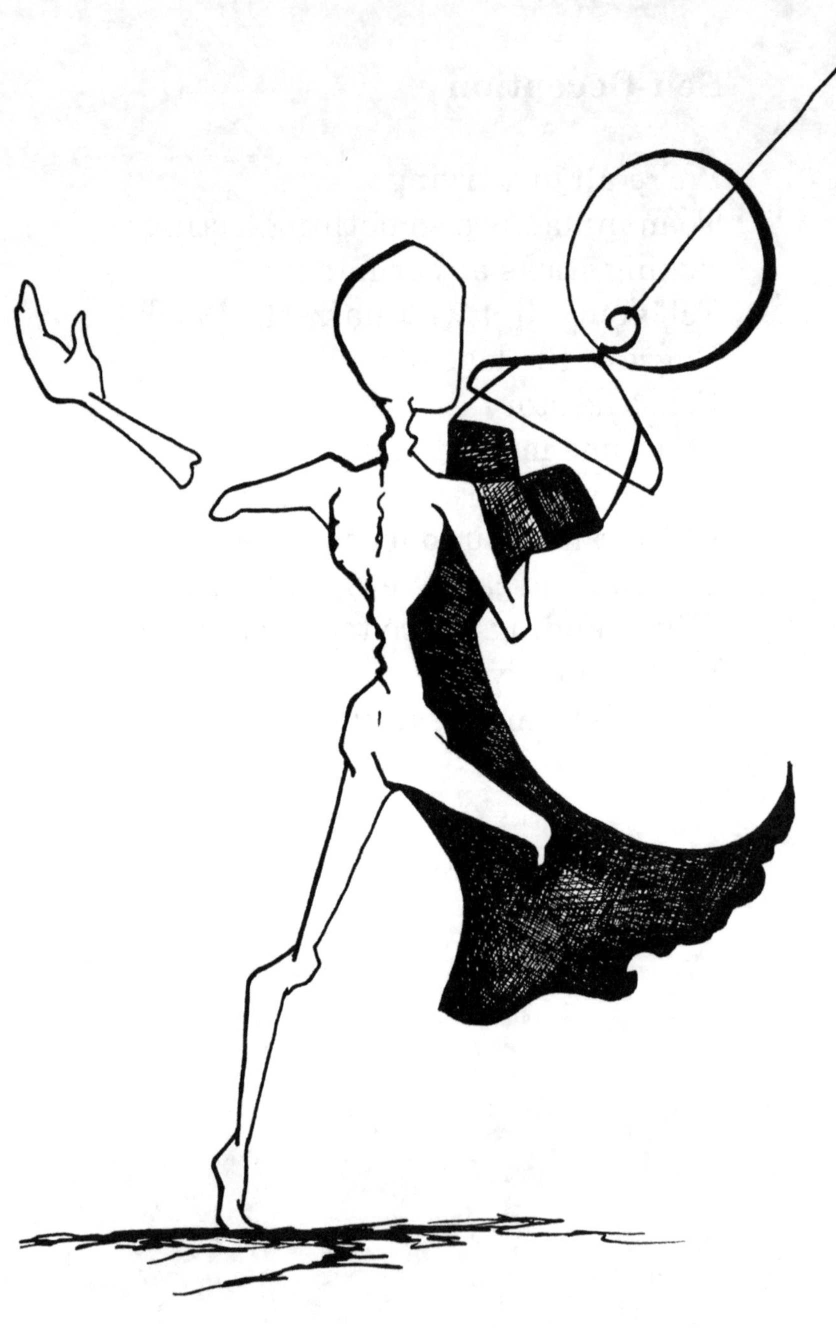

Act 1

Brutal ballet
Solitary stage
An audience of vacancy
Self-immolating imagination
Panic against complacency

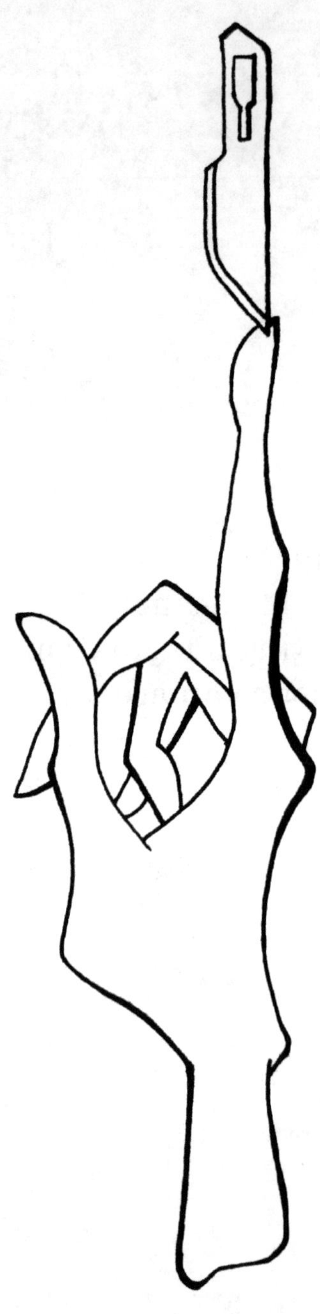

Love Songs

Every love story lied
Filled your head
With fatal advice
Wrong expectations
Unreal exaltations
Prescription failure
Heartbreak and despair
Unrecognizable truth
Manipulation Monopoly
Keep passing go
They taught you disease

Suck It

Is it brilliant
Or is it shit
Is it art
Or should I quit
I can't tell
Nobody knows
You might like it
I think it blows
It doesn't matter
Not one fuck
Keep making stuff
Even when it sucks

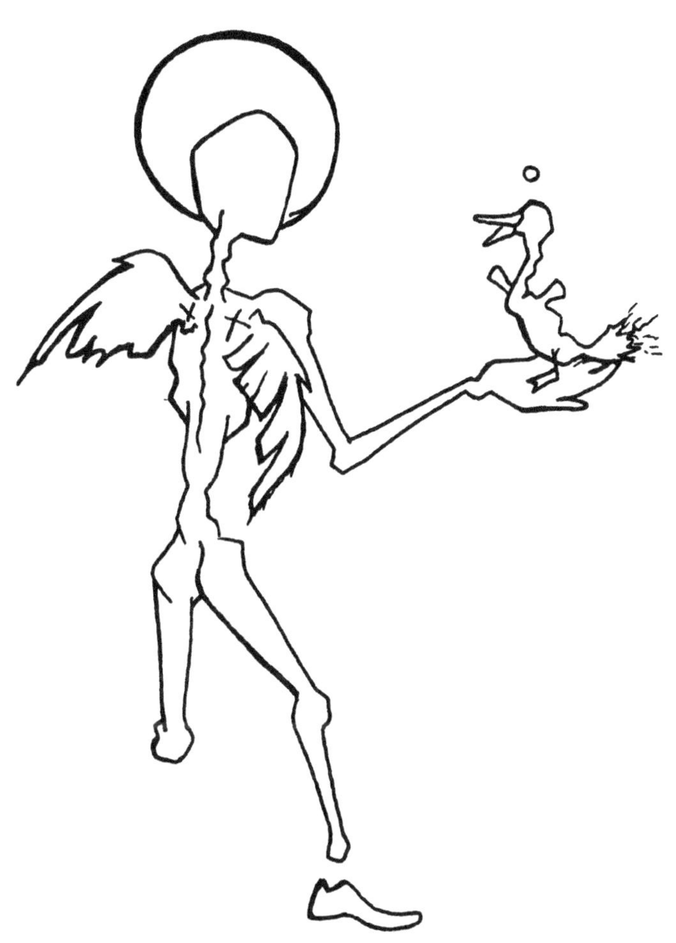

Content Warning

How do you live
When there's nothing to fight
Is it a life
When your mind is alright

Why should I worry
Content doesn't last long
Pain waits in the silence
At the end of the song

Darkness will creep
We'll be back where we started
Let down by it all
And thoroughly disheartened

So find something smiling
Then burn it on down
Live in the loss
Hold on to the sound

I've Seen This Episode Before

Flashbacks
Rerun pain tracks
One little trip switch
Terror hums a low pitch
Lose my will to fight
The dark is just too bright
Erase so many years
Of struggle work and tears
Building something sort of human
But in a second here again
I'm right back to year two
Yes, I do remember you
You likely don't think of it much
I'm ruined again by your touch

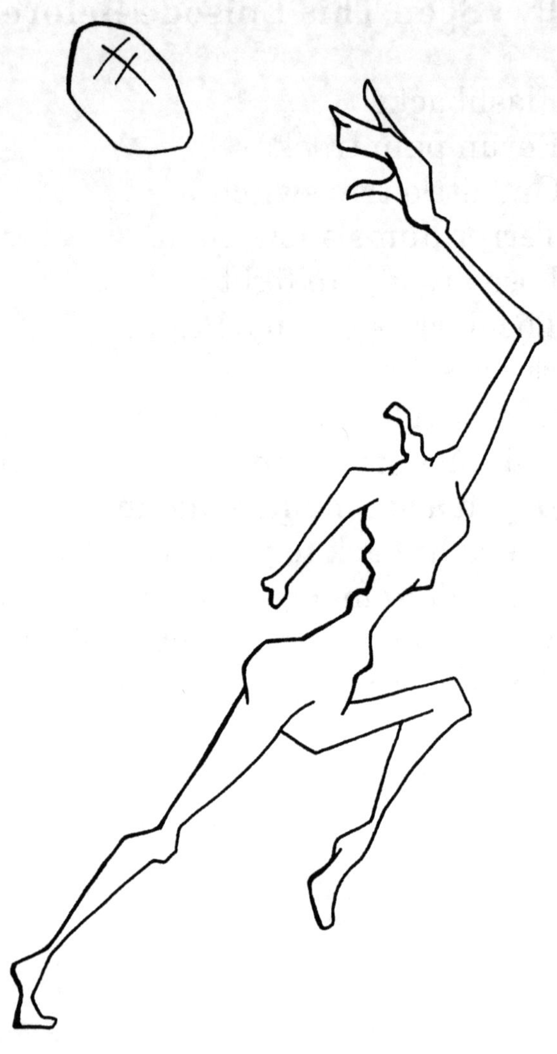

Why

Worthless words
On a failing page
Pathetic mumbling
On an empty stage
Applause changes nothing
It's still a lie
A monkey babbling
Before it dies

Bitte

Despite the begging and the pleading
The cold comes in and I'm still bleeding

You

I painted your face
In the name of art
Called it that
To cover the fact
That I just wanted
To look at you
I sold your face
To someone who
Wanted you too
I painted your face again
In the name of profit
Another good excuse
To spend some time
With the idea of you
I'll paint your face
In the name of love
A hundred times
Until nothing's left
Except
  For you

Psych

I had a therapist
Back in the day
If he read this
I know what he'd say

Goodnight

I used to dream of screaming
Desperate to awake
Tortured nerves piano strings
The tune is death and failure
I used to fear the night
What pain that I'd inflict
And now I dream of loving
Tender touch and gentle word
A face gaze down smiling sweetly
I have no need to doubt
Now I want to sleep forever
In safe and warm embrace
I used to dream of screaming
Now I do it when I wake

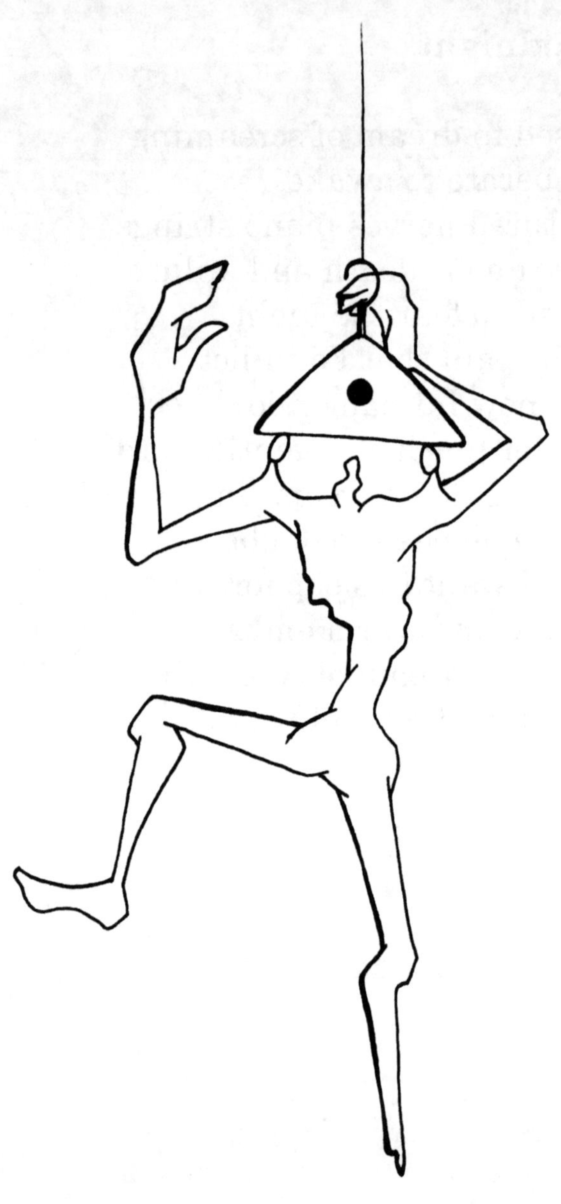

Accomplishments

You pretend to be important
Make an impact on the world
We know the truth is disappointing
Don't let it say the word

Nothing matters let's be honest
Time forgets every witness
Suffering is without a purpose
Self-deception has to do

Tell yourself you're making something
Worth the price of your existence
It's a lie as all things are
I'll keep it silent if you will too

Future

Hell is silent
And the night is violent
Little girls with holes inside
Mourning for the parts that died

Undecided

I don't really want to die
You know it's coming for me anyway
No use helping it along
Might as well hang on and stay

I don't really want to be here
You know I haven't done that much
Maybe I'll just sleep a while
Till my skin is cold to touch

Either way who really cares
I'm forgotten here or dead
You'll be gone in good time too
With all the things we wish we'd said

Safe

Lonesome is no price to pay
To no longer be betrayed
Rather sit with myself in silence
Than justify your misplaced violence

One can learn to love the ache
The wound that isolations make
To no more so bear your fear
Though time is slow, it's safer here

Soon it seems that I prefer it
This cage I've made so dimly lit
I wonder if I've just forgotten
The smell of what is not yet rotten

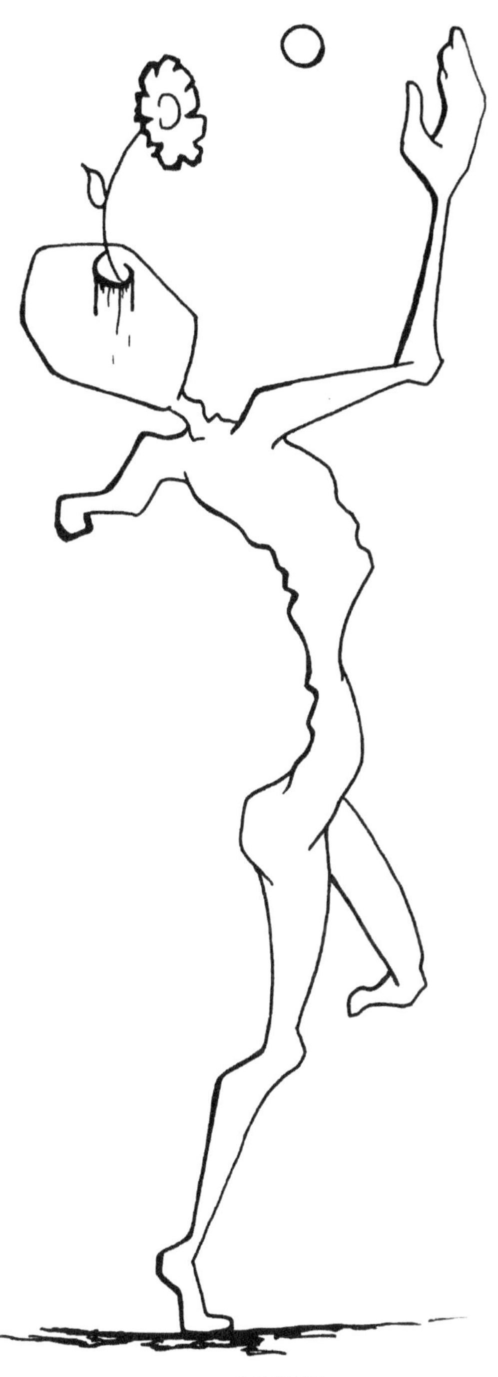

Looking Forward

Time rolls on
Light will grow
We with hope
Still yet know
None will notice
Once we go

Lucky No. 9

Chop chop
Down to nine
Save myself
For better times

Digit lingers
In a jar
Messer hardly
Left a scar

Lucky number
Proves I can
Terror died
And life began

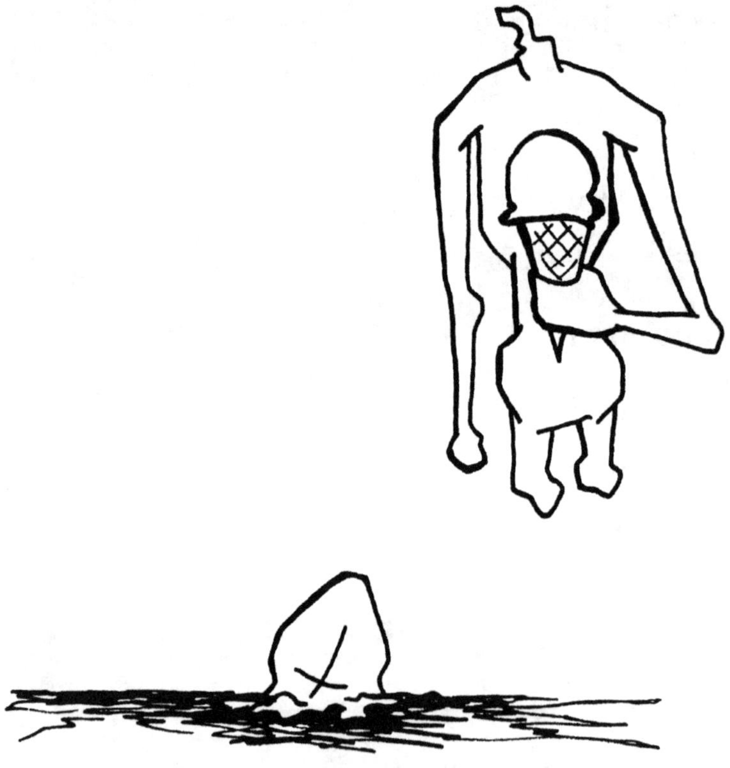

The Let Down

Set a goal you'll never reach
Doesn't matter what it is
Trick yourself into moving forward
Never leave it standing still

If you do you'll soon discover
Nothing's real and nothing matters
We scream and flail a little while
Die in silence and are forgotten

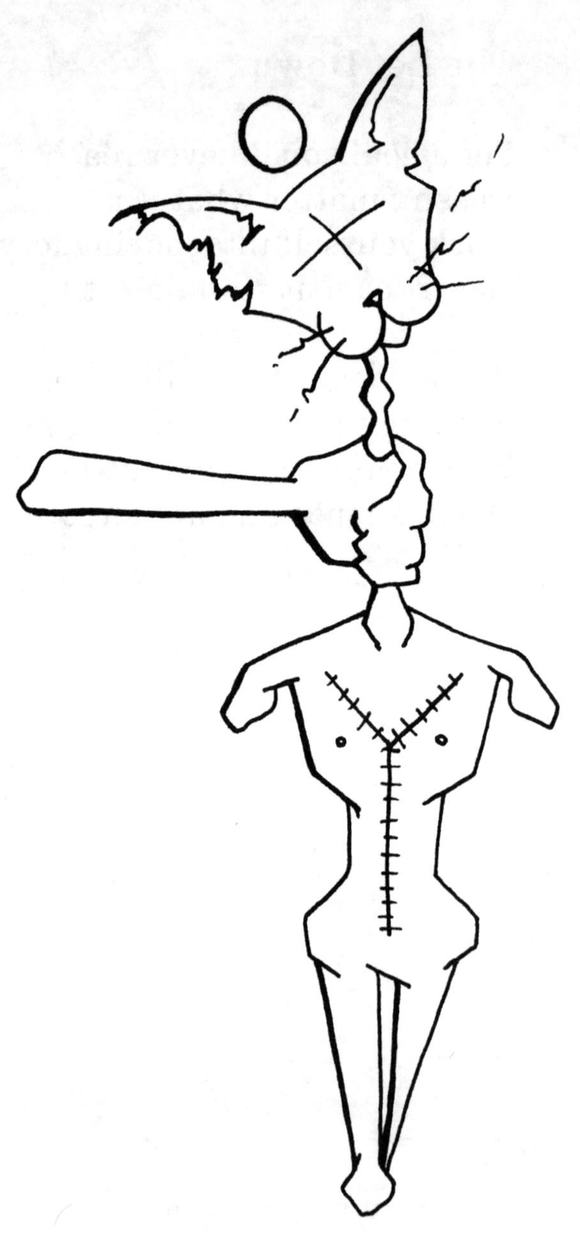

Do Over

Put your hands around my throat
I want to enjoy it this time

Red Song

When everything is calm and soundless
The echoes call from out the forest
I take the sharp and shining
And strike the tune that can't be quiet

It plays the skin with rise and fall
Light it beads and loud in streams
Fresh notes drip and old ones stick
Smeared on skin the thing's a mess

When the singing's finally over
It dries so fast in crust and blackness
I can't remember how it sounded
Nothing's left but hot white silence

You Fill the Blank

I feel a lot of things for you
Not sure if they are love
I don’t want you to hurt or die
But really now I can’t say why

I'd like if you would stick around
I'm afraid to see you go
It's not really you I need
I have a hole that you can feed

Tea Party

The other kids
Won't come to play
I don't know why
Who can say
The tea is hot
Crumpets fresh
And china clean
My favorite friends
Are here already
Sitting pretty
If a bit unsteady
I found them early
With most their pieces
Don't smell too bad
But the bunny's leaking
When these friends
Can't drink their tea
I'll get some more
On highway three
One day the kids
Will see our fun
They'll come to join
Instead of run

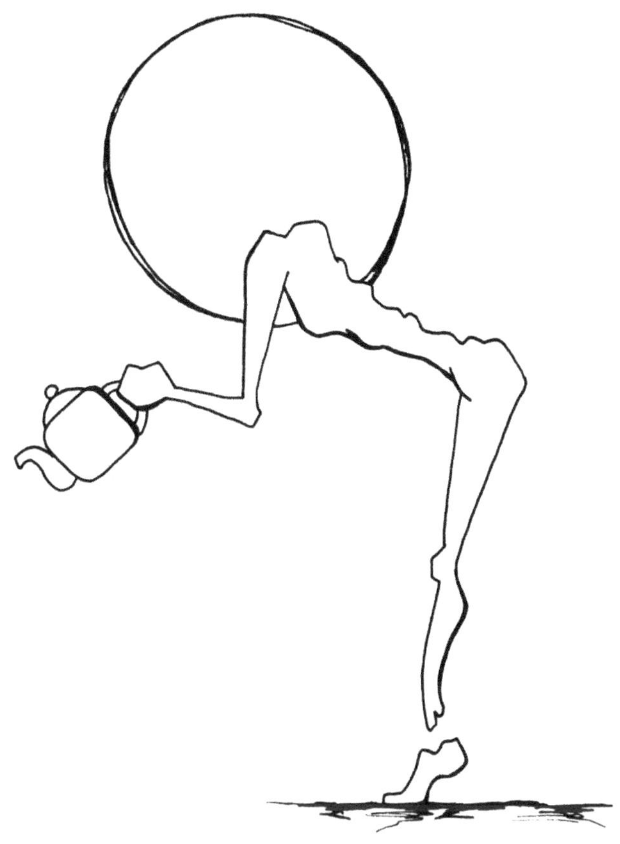

Family

The only blood
That's ever mattered
Is self-contained
Sometimes splattered

Disconnected

Something's rotten
In the center
Not forgotten
Just neglected

Leave the lid on
Fastened tightly
Injection drawn
It's infected

What's hidden stays
For a while
It all decays
Gone uncorrected

Let them in
They turn away
The smell of sin
Is unexpected

Black

I'm afraid
I've got no more
Every drop
Is on the floor

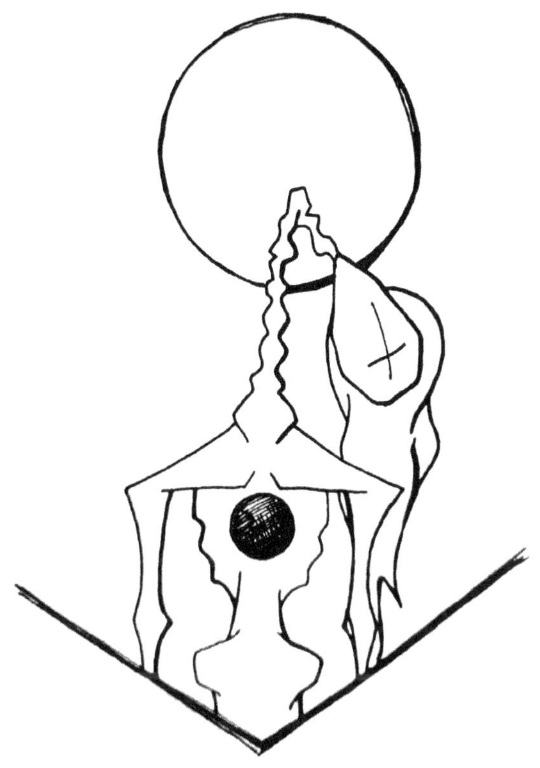

How

What will I be
When the nightmares are gone
What will I do
When nothing is wrong

Sit in a chair
And stare at the wall
Is that what you do
When the demons fall

How will I know
When content wanders in
How do I bear it
When it's under my skin

Oblivious

Demons dress like people
And they tell me
That they love me

Cut my throat in tiny slices
I do not notice
I'm bleeding out

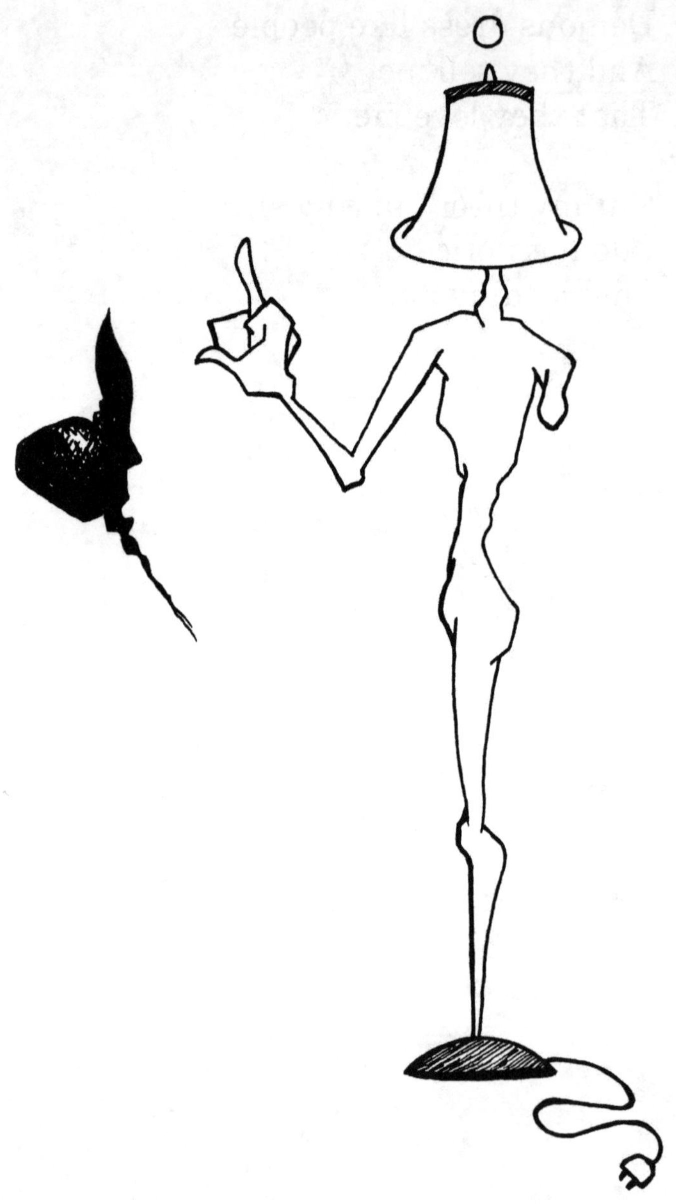

Dramatic Production

Souls will scream
And tears will riot
For all our wailing
Death comes quiet

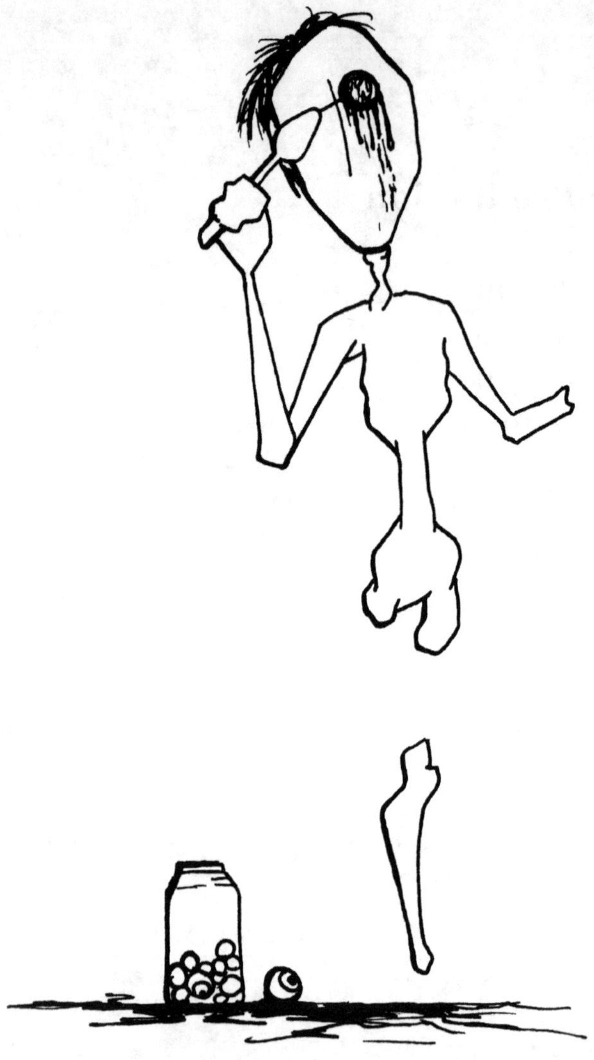

Kindness

Hit me hard
Leave a mark
Hold me after
In gentle dark
Hate me brightly
Rend my heart
Whisper softly
We'll never part
Make me beg
For your relief
Smile falsely
Blood slick teeth
Destroy me kindly
So none remains
Remember love
Look how it stains

Yes

All your life is spent searching
For someone to say yes
To fill the sucking hole and question
Drive it from your heart's contention
Finally a solid answer
Ineffable but plainly clear
A nodding to your sad existence
This is just as it should happen
Worry not for random chances
Choices follow to the plan
Each direction leads to rightness
Believe it true while cold you shiver
Left alone out in the blizzard
Slowly as your blood goes solid
Vision fades while still seeking
That one word all resounding
Say it to yourself, lips cracking
Was all this just for nothing

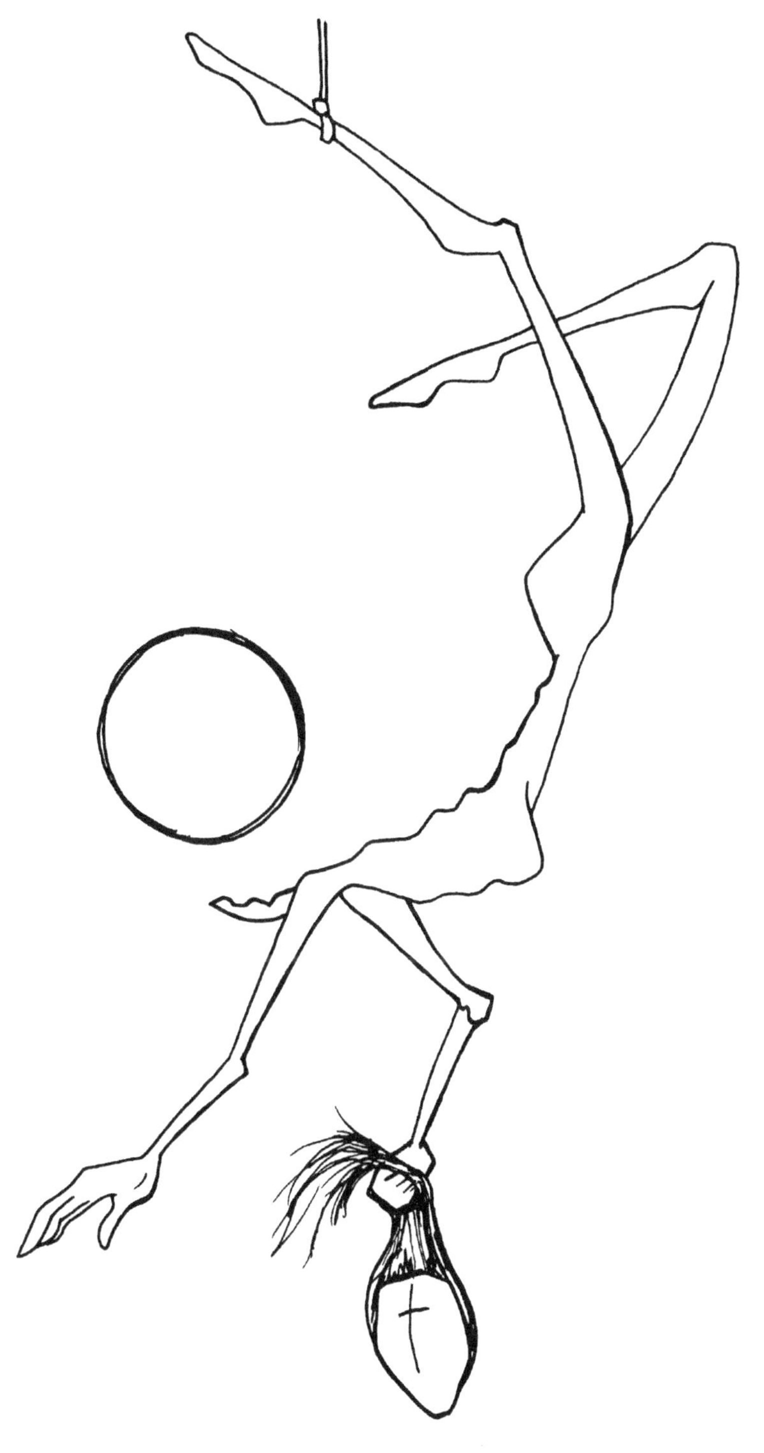

Try

If you're not making
You're only taking
Manic manufacturing
To prove there is a point
Ten thousand tries
In corners and closets
Sell you my failures
And eat your pity
Spend my life in attemptation
It only hurts
I can't sit still

No

Dreams come true
Just not for you

Leaks

Drippings of a broken person
Melted hoping slips away
What remains is no body
Unused future left for rotting

It sticks and stings
As light leaks from you
Heart disease for hidden sins
No savior comes when it begins

Life is flowing redly downward
Slowly toward the dirt we go
Infected early and broken later
Only lies can promise greater

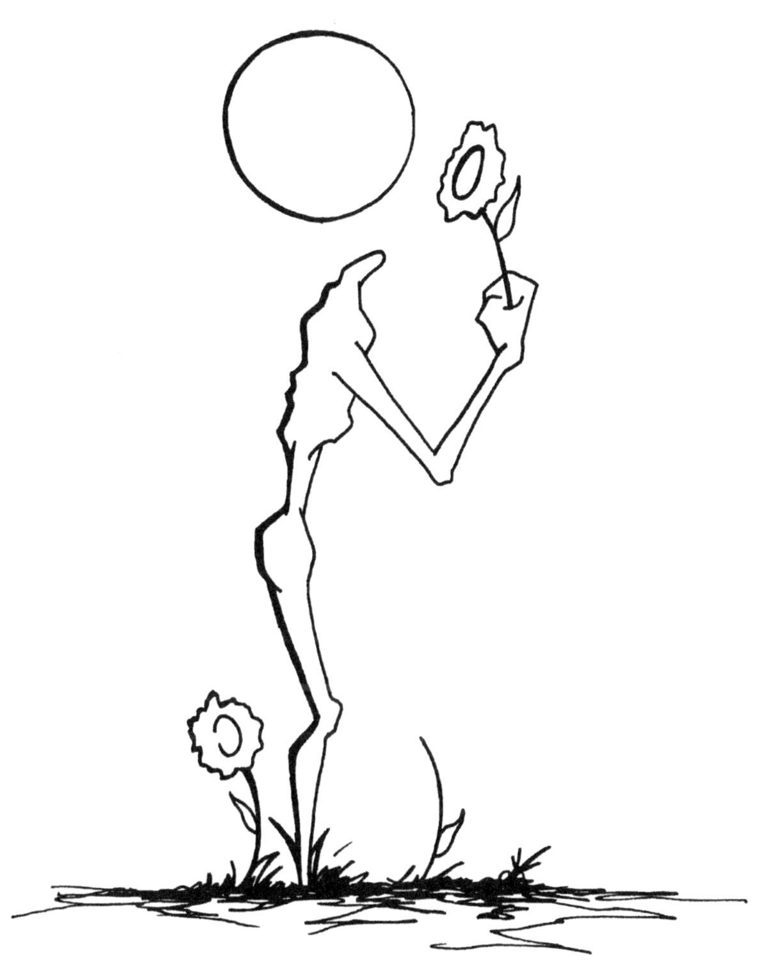

Mine

The trick
Is to accept
What's coming
Don't fight
It now
Just let it
Take you
Struggle only
Makes me
Hurt you
I don't
Want to
Hear the
Screaming
Quiet comes
So very quickly
Thumbs upon
Beating artery
Peace is warm
Vision fading
Swim away
So I can
Keep you

Relationship

Fuck me up
Dick me down
Call me pretty
Don't fuck around

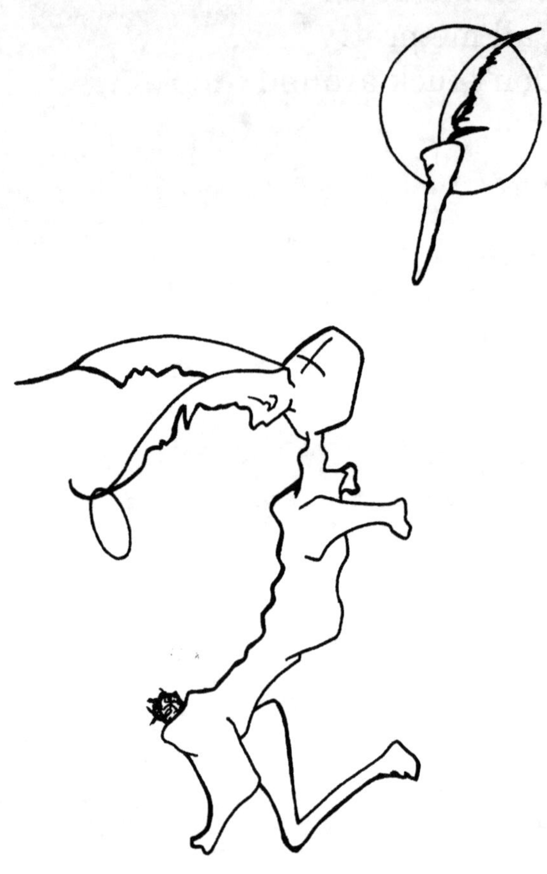

Service Fee

Red pearls swell until
Can no longer sit still
Under their own weight
They must roll
Downhill over gooseflesh
Delicate hairs at attention
No hindrance now
For rolling redness
Painting trails of living wetness
A few drops less inside
Doubt skulks off again defeated
Take your life outside
And view it
Life is costly
But blood flows freely

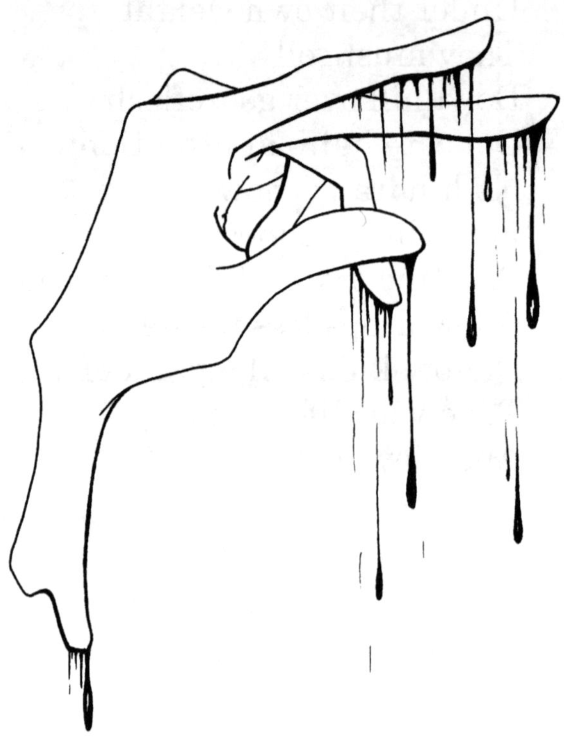

Hearts

Turn the light on
Click like on me
Give me a little reason
To continue to be

Tell your friends
To fill me up too
I'm vacant inside
I need it from you

I like what you see
Fuck what I am
I'll live in your eyes
We're both in the scam

Peace

There's a certain kind of silence
Only frozen night can bring
Beating hearts dare not break it
Still in the moonlight fears to sing

Frostbite calls for movement
Without voice or lending hand
But held in place by perfect quiet
Deceptive kindness, fatal land

Temptation whispers join us
Diamonds glitter on the snow
Beauty seeps into the center
As the blood begins to slow

Rohheit

When in the light
Eyes begin to burn
Then so in night
Tears douse in turn

Numbing hearts will crack
Against wishes not to feel
Darkness always gives it back
All damage to reveal

Overtaken by the hidden things
No longer halted by the day
Illness waking spreads its wings
Always leads you far astray

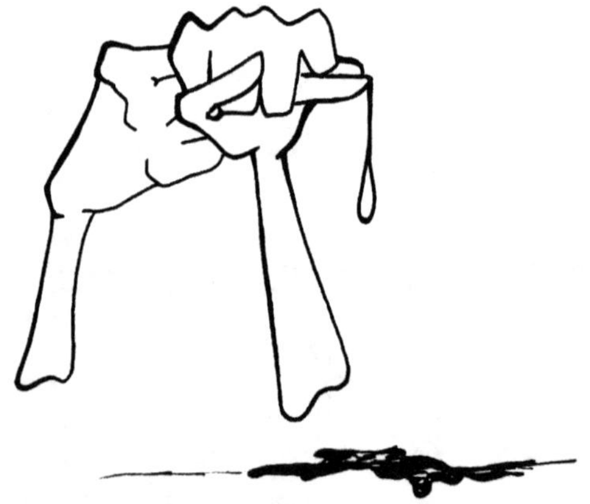

Plastik

For all the talk of wailing, screaming
I really don't feel much at all
Maybe it's just wishful thinking
Torture's better than numb to all

Something grand and dramatic
Proves this thing has some meaning
Fighting desperate for a cause
Nothing matters when blood is streaming

Make it well and I'll believe it
Production cost is life soon ending
All the clanging fills the silence
Plastic feelings in heart contending

Epiphany

Beauty lies
Goodness dies
Evil wins
Rich man grins
We remain
Yet in pain
Life decays
Deception pays

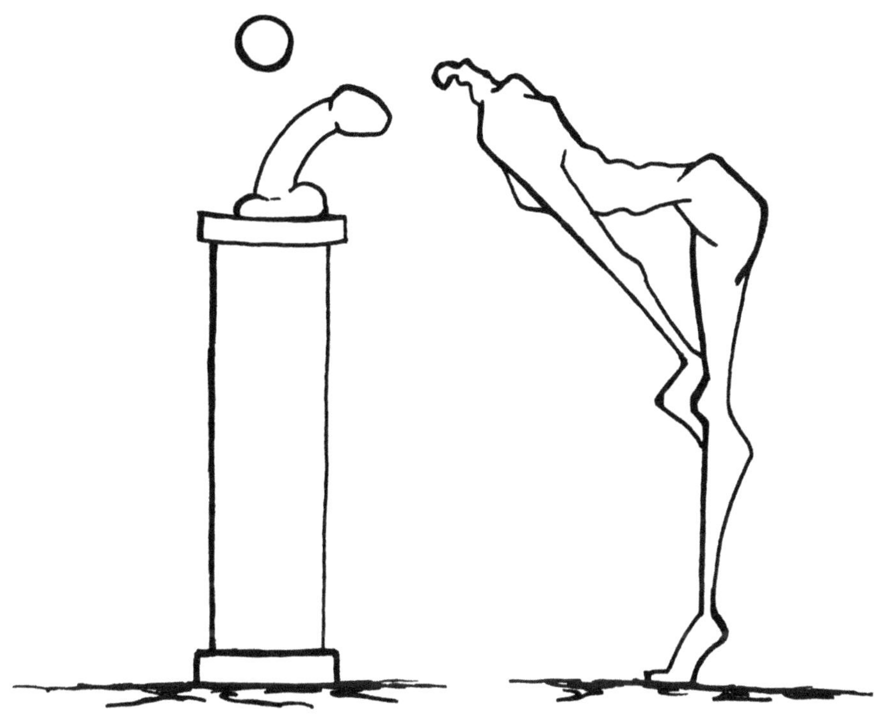

Expired

Evening burns away
Fresh moods begin to black
Bloodshot in a room
When sense is coming back

The ones you once admired
Decay into graven faces
Too much everything
Chasing bright in bloody races

Goodness curdles ever sour
Warping melodies in song
Watch them scratch in desperation
Growing light and shadows long

Forever round they go
Too ashamed to see it now
Infection spreads among them
And they barely wonder how

Whimper

Silence grinds until it's raw
The beast bit down and broke its jaw
Sun falls off and turns to grey
Rage castrated begs to stay

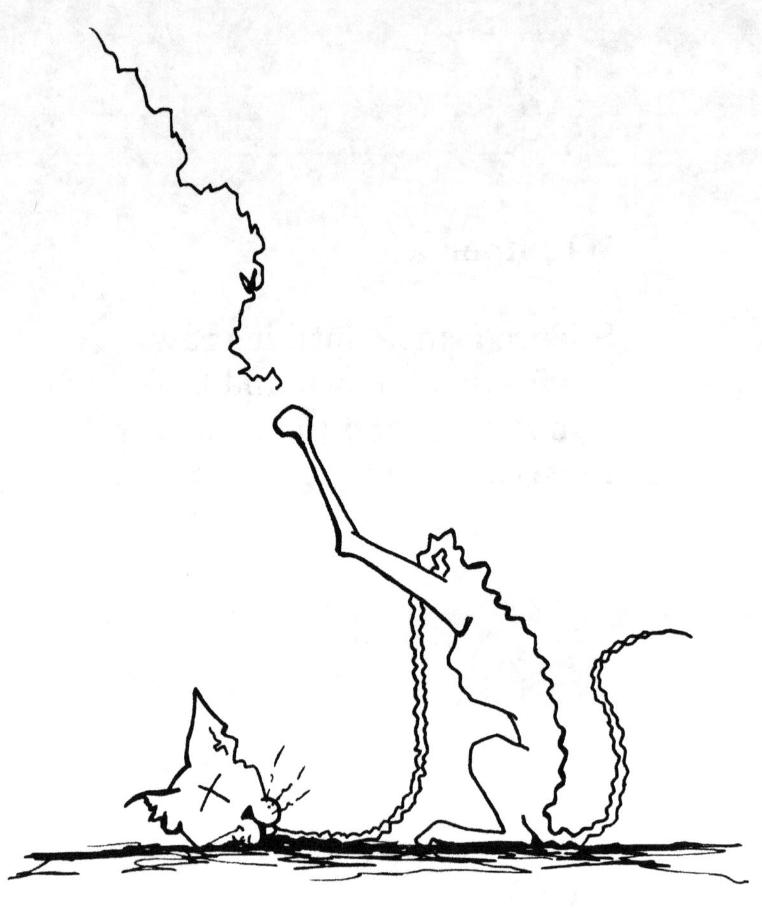

Cause and Effect

Trace the cracks along the skin
So far back where they begin
Deep cut in it burrows down
Built on sand the bones unsound

Walk unsteady through the mud
Stagnant wreckage of the flood
Though we can now name the cause
Scars still raise up from our flaws

Stitches mend us from disaster
From inside wounds open faster
Can't repair condemned foundation
No choice is left but amputation

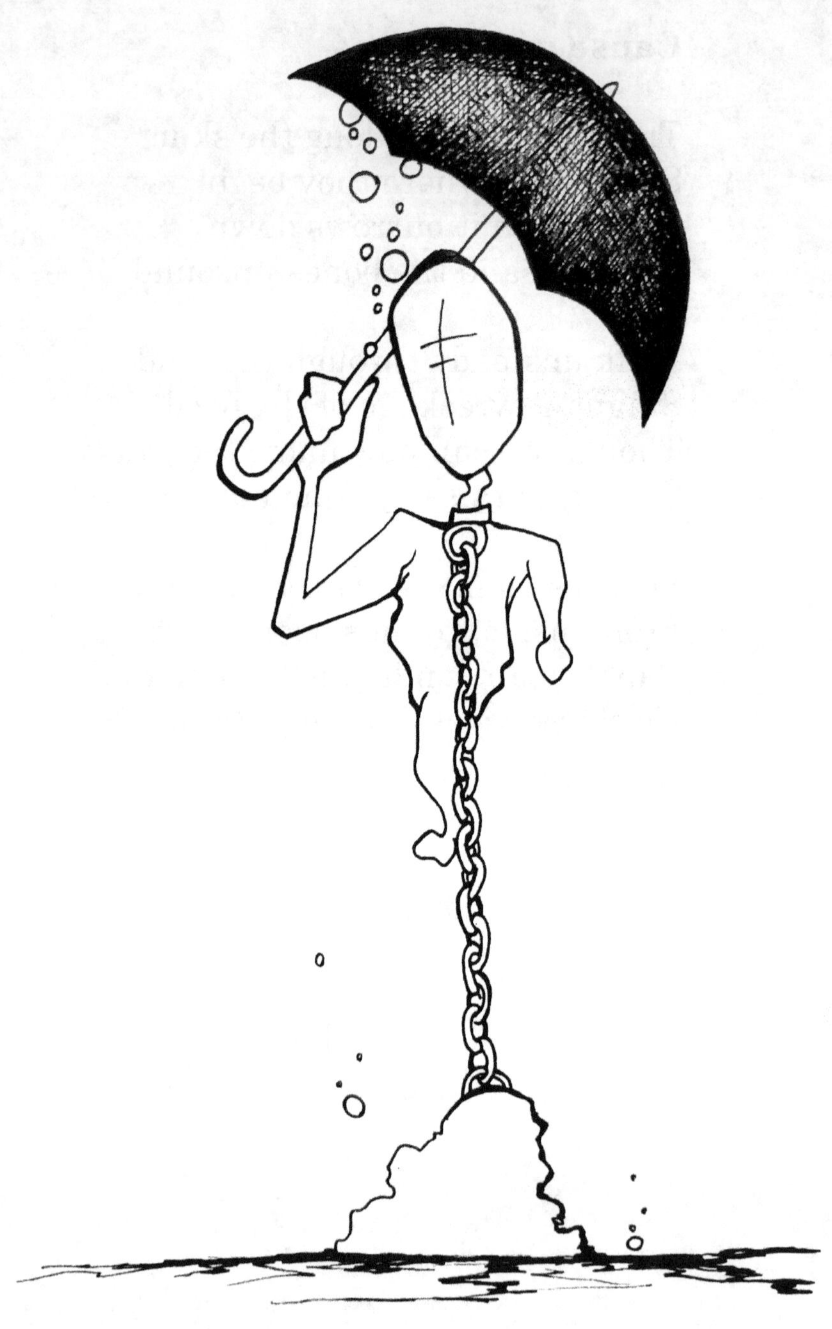

Reality

Please don't ever
Come to me
And ruin what I have
Made you be

Temporary

How many tries
Should it take
Inward facing lies
For sanity's sake
The time it buys
Before accepting fate
To love and be likewise
A heart sits stagnate

Albernheit

Да, ja, yes, sí, oui
Wir wissen jetzt nicht wie
Просто немного да и радости
Yes so here we go, a reason yet to be!

Please

Miss the mark every time
Reaching for a hand
Contact never made
Touch that never lands
Phantoms of connection
Seen but never felt
An absent thing for longing
Somehow leaves a welt
Are we all without it
Pretending not to see
There has to be another
Don't let it just be me

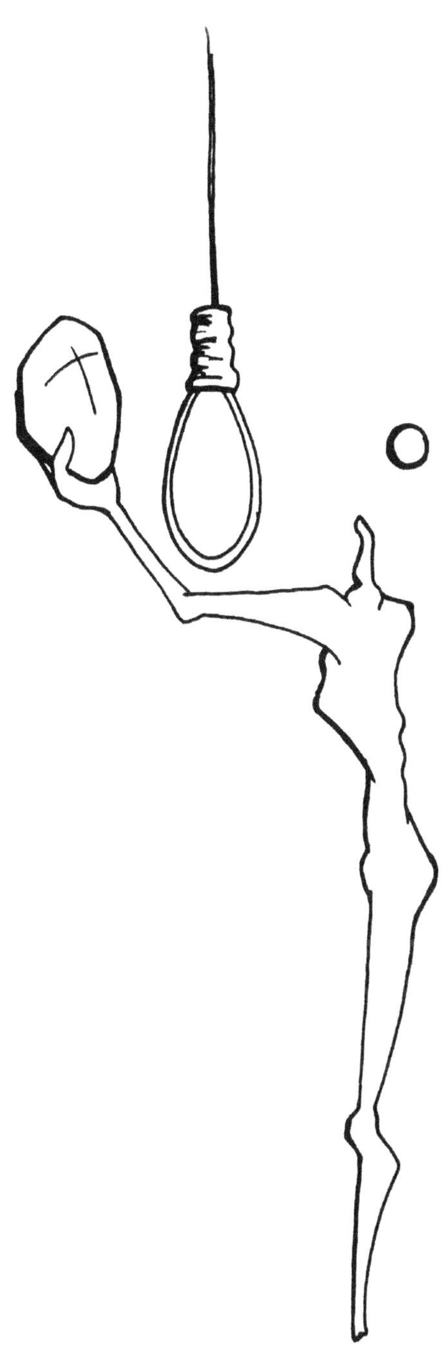

Merry Go Round

Every day to my surprise
Sunlight greets my open eyes
A death and then again a life
Some sip of joy despite the strife

So once again around it goes
The workings cruel and so exposed
Yet still the desperate game is played
And at the end our souls are weighed

How any make it out enlightened
Despite a hundred years spent frightened
Knowing secretly it's just a ruse
Every heartbeat leaves a bruise

A wind-up toy worn out till broken
The music slows, I'm out of tokens
Smoke is drifting toward the skies
But once again light burns my eyes

Selfie

If you look deep enough
Into the camera you're holding
You might find someone
To cure your self- loathing

Bullet's Prayer

In the name of
The Bother
The Gun
And the Wholly Toast

Reload,
        Again

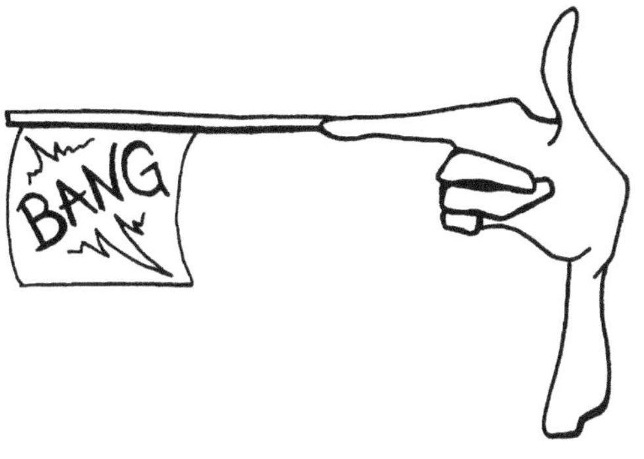
BANG

Eventually

Accept the vacancy you live
Once you have no more to give
If you've forgotten how to die
She'll come to see you by the by

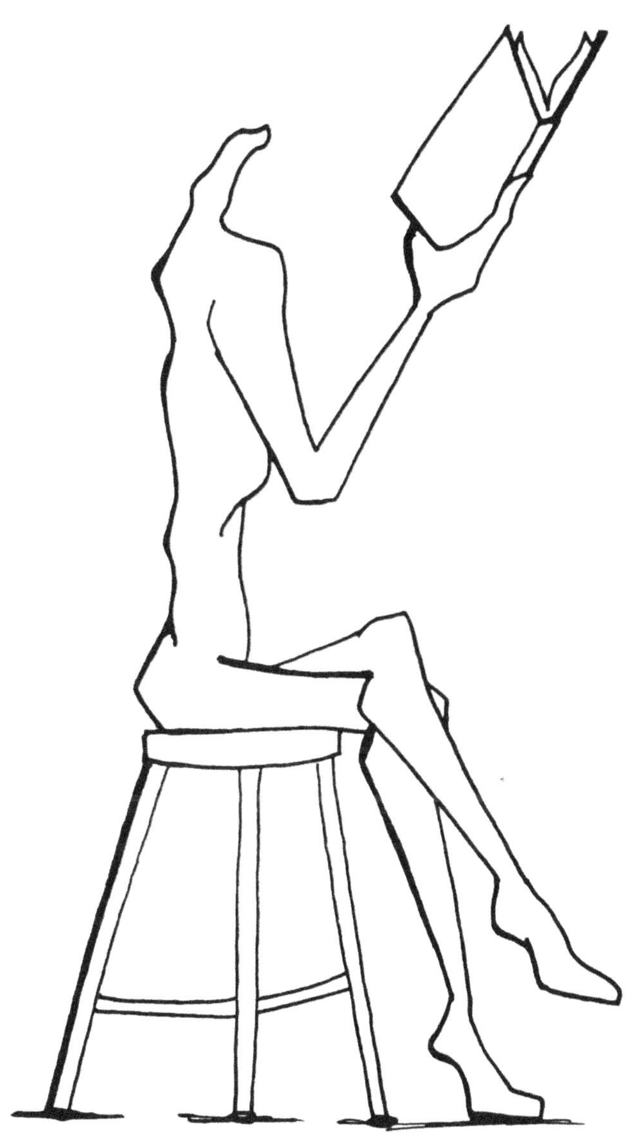

Individual

Seven billion souls
Wanting to be heard
Scrounging in the dirt
For a single unused word

Time remembers nothing
Heart beating drips away
Hurricanes fall dead at sea
No light nor warmth can stay

To eyes that see the self
Each reflection is unique
Seven billion mirrors shine
Giving in to what we seek

Hope

Nothing lasts
But we still prefer
Leaving something
To prove we were

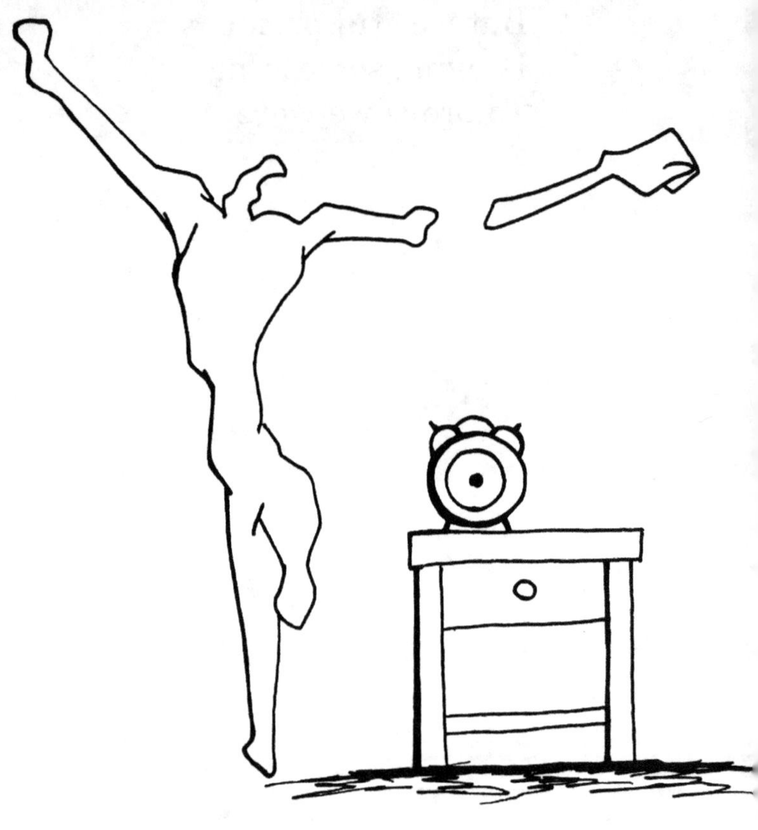

Herzloch

Es gibt
Messer
Für der Esser
Gebenden
Für das Lebenden
Auch
Hiebenden
Für das Liebenden

Introspection

I don't know
If words will last

I'm just blowing smoke
Right out my ass

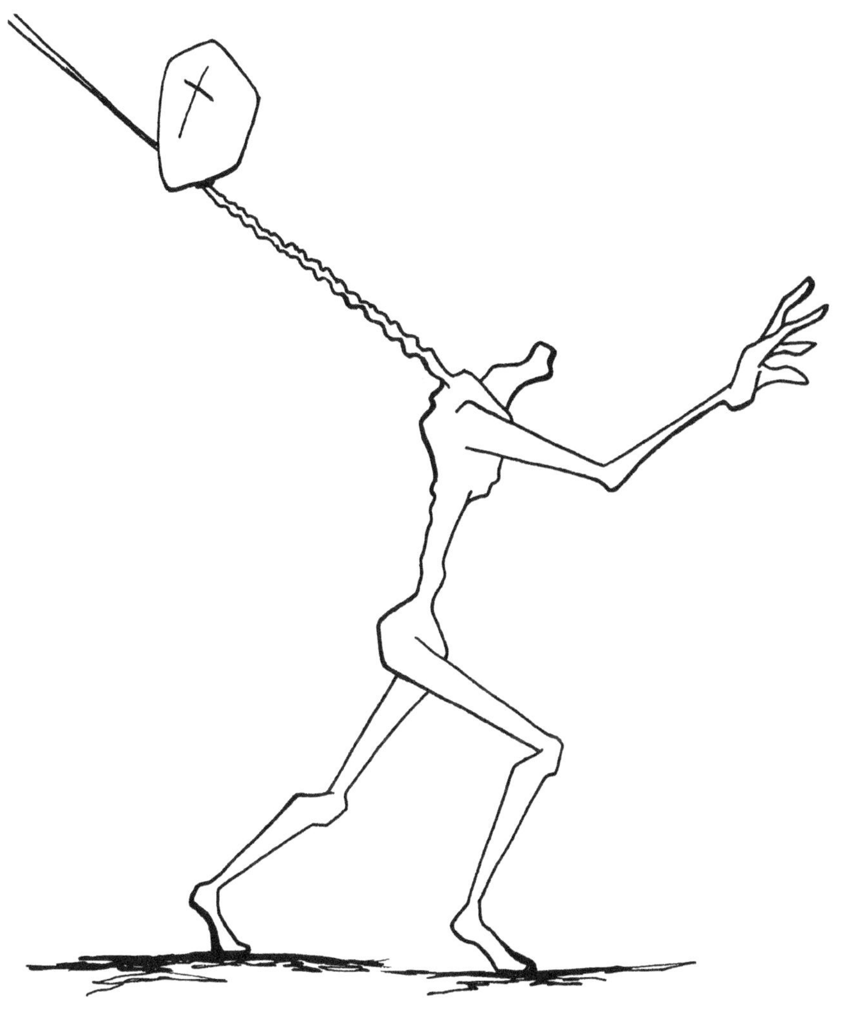

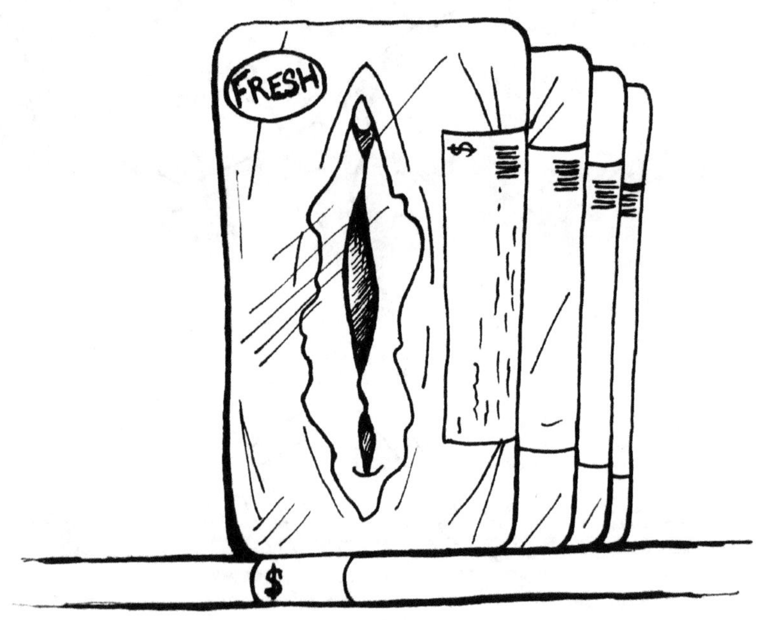
FRESH

Needs

To win your love
Each one is trying
Who says they're not
Is always lying

Shithead Undercover

Can't you
See us
Dirty Kids
We are
The Ones
With holes
In our shirts
And our boots
In our faces
And our souls

Nein

In the end
With any luck
There will be someone
Who gave a fuck

You'll likely find
Before you go
To questions asked
The answer's no

Trout

Silence spreads its arms so wide
And welcomes those with void inside
The song plays out in absent sound
Guiding us, the downward bound

The message speaks between the beats
A thing that grows and only eats
Matches up with what we lack
Shaped like things we can't get back

All along a life it follows
Not unreal but made of hollow
Without us onward river flows
Each drop's lament sings
So It Goes

Нахуй

Я плохо знаю русский
Но я все равно пытаюсь
я глупый
На четырех языках

Endlich

Every bit was meant for you
Though neither of us ever knew

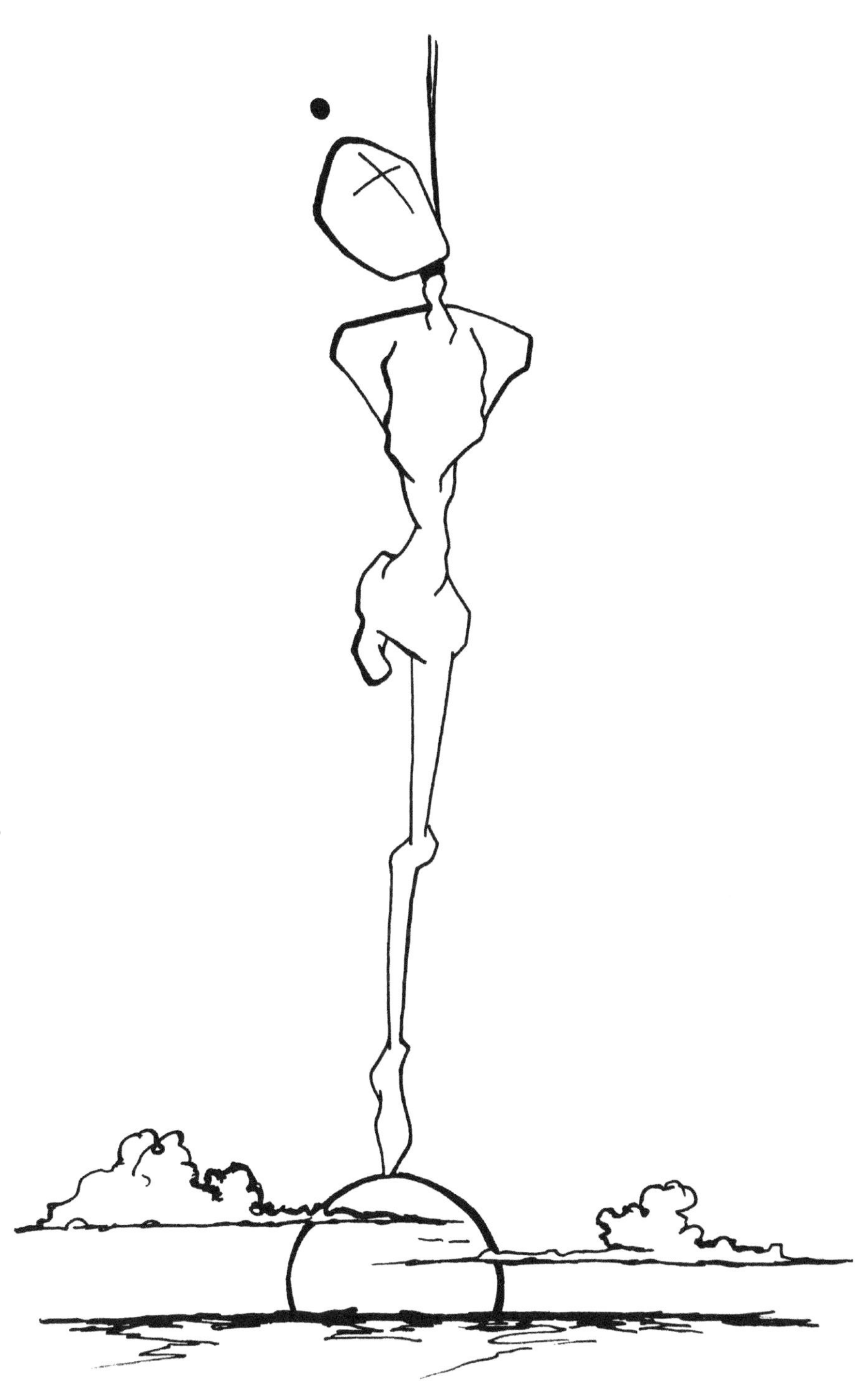

Index

Index

Index

For Samm Bones

Without you this book would not have been possible
Without you I am not possible
Я люблю тебя

www.ingramcontent.com/pod-product-compliance
Lightning Source LLC
LaVergne TN
LVHW050537100826
845148LV00002B/593

9780578609126